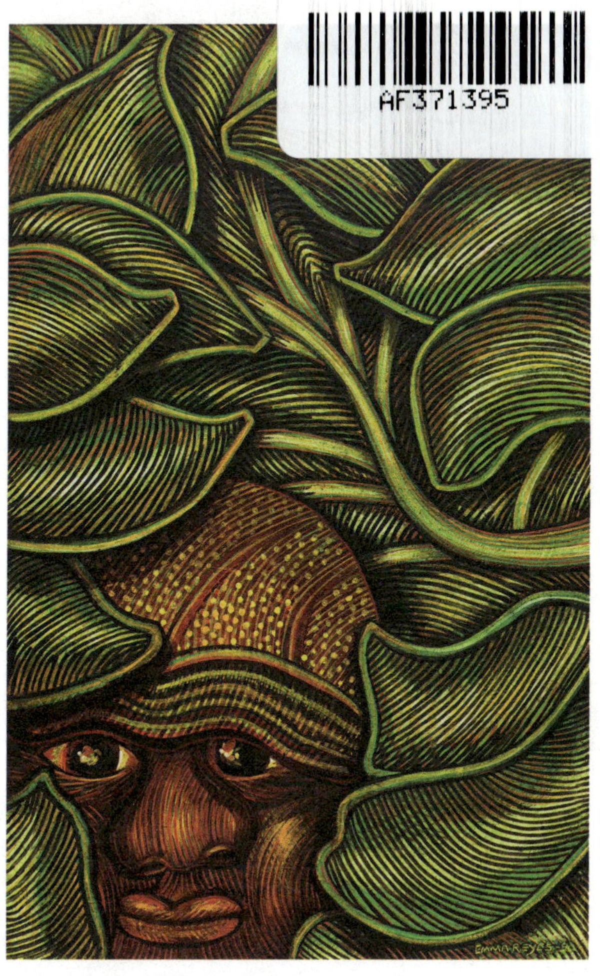

Untitled, 1990
Acrylic paint on canvas, 100 × 75 cm

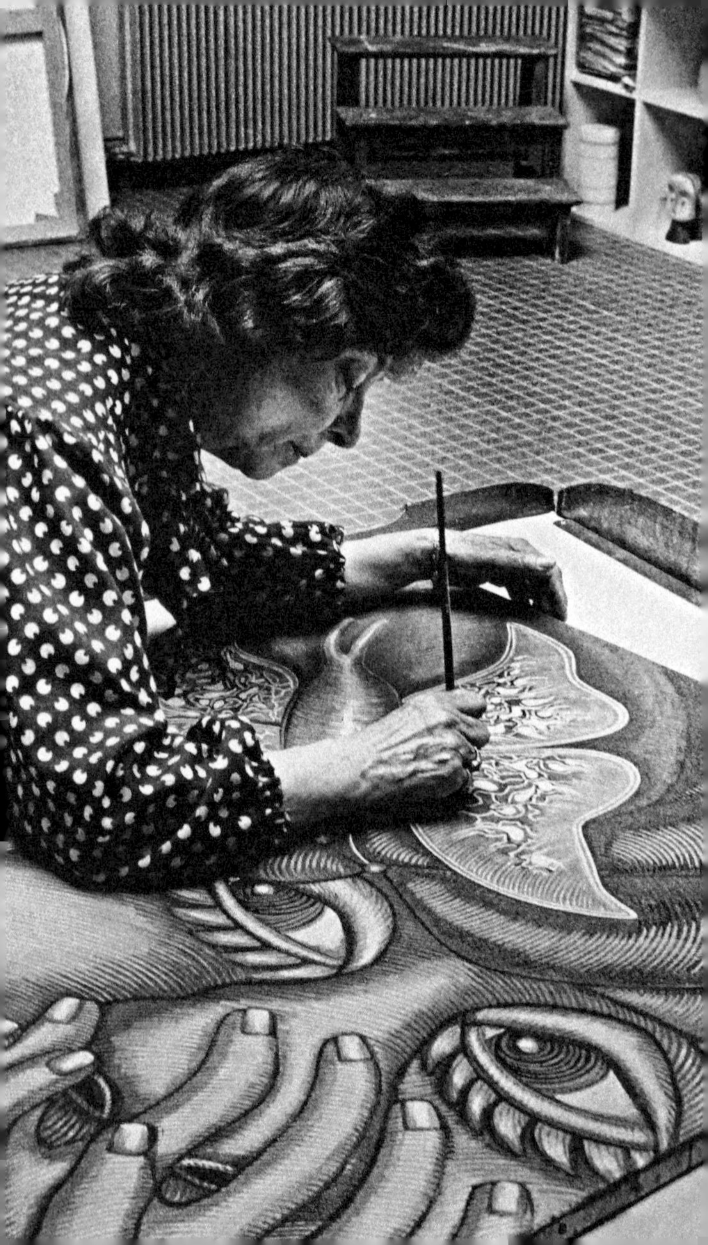

Emma Reyes

Stéphanie Cottin (ed.)

jrp|editions

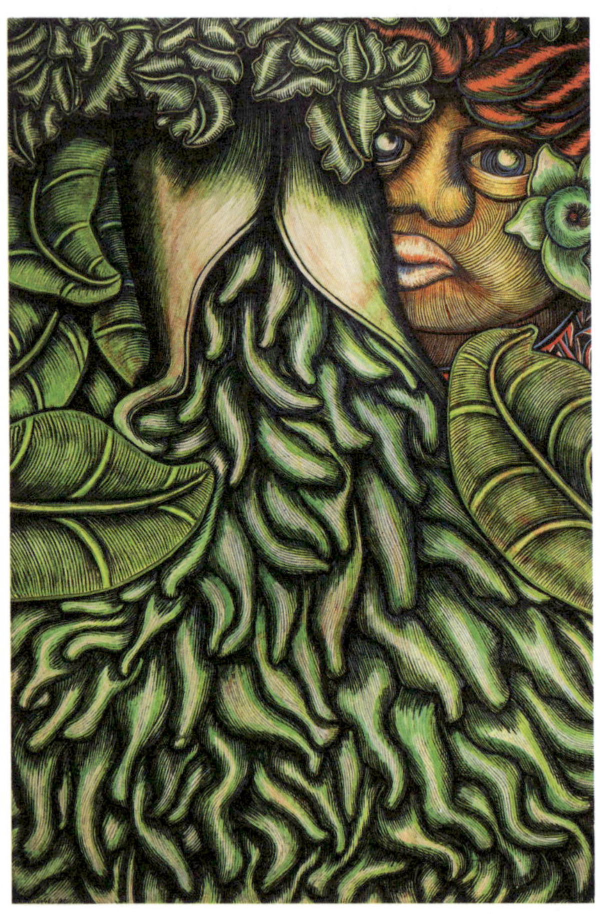

Omaira, 1985
Acrylic paint on canvas, 200 × 135 cm

← Emma Reyes in her studio, Paris, c. 1980

Emma Reyes' Vegetation as a Force of Change

Miguel A. López

The life and work of Emma Reyes (1919–2003) have achieved legendary status. Her creative practice started to gain global attention after the publication of her memoir, a series of letters to her friend, the Colombian historian and journalist Germán Arciniegas (1900–1999). These letters, discovered posthumously, were first published in Spanish in 2012, and translated into English and French in 2017.[1] They offer a glimpse into her vibrant imagination as a young girl, and the profound influence of her upbringing in poverty in a Catholic convent. These challenges, coupled with her insatiable curiosity, propelled her to embrace painting in order to explore the diverse realities and places she encountered.

However, even though her persona has recently begun attracting the attention of writers and researchers, it is a stark reality that little literature or studies, and very few exhibitions, have been dedicated to her art. Beyond obituaries and short press reviews, her death in

Bordeaux in 2003 remained mainly unnoticed in her native Colombia, where many of her paintings and drawings have been largely absent from local art history books. This underappreciation of her art is a testament to the fact that in a space and time when masculine values dominate, hybrid artistic vocabularies like hers (and those of many other female artists) that do not fit into recognized versions of the modernist canon have usually been rendered invisible.

Reyes' migration across multiple sites was a defining mark of her creative trajectory. She left Colombia at 20 to travel overland in South America, taking on small jobs to make ends meet. Her passion for painting began during her displacement between Argentina and Paraguay in the early and mid 1940s. As a self-taught painter with limited knowledge of art history, she sought to be close to other artists. Having settled back in Buenos Aires in 1947, she worked as an assistant with the renowned realist painter Antonio Berni (1905–1981). With a scholarship, she traveled to Paris in 1947 to study under the Cubist painter André Lhote (1885–1962). In 1949, she held her first solo exhibition at the Galerie Kléber in Paris. In 1952, she moved to Mexico, where she worked in the studios of Diego Rivera (1886–1957) and photographer

Lola Álvarez Bravo (1903–1993). After living in many places, she eventually settled in Paris in 1960. Reyes' restless nature and wide-ranging perspective allowed her to engage creatively with the cultural atmosphere in all these places, sparking various forms of conversation with her contemporaries through her painting.

Reyes' mature work emerged in the mid-1950s in Rome when she began creating a series of small oil, ink, and watercolor portraits. Many of these were titled "Monstres" (Monsters), depicting hybrids of animals and humans, somehow akin to the drawings from the "Masques" (Masks) series she created from the 1990s until shortly before her death. These works were influenced by pre-Columbian sources and artifacts such as Mexica culture ceramics, while also reflecting her desire to explore intense emotional states and subjectivity. In the 1960s she experimented with various forms of abstraction, including drawings and paintings made of delicate geometric and curved lines. However, she returned to her focus on the human figure in the 1970s.

Reyes created her initial drawings for the series "Portraits Imaginaires" (Imaginary Portraits) using black India ink on paper. She crafted intricate three-dimensional heads against backgrounds resembling textile patterns, paying particular attention to the hair and facial features. Shortly after, the artist transferred the idea of these portraits onto large-scale canvases, which resulted in lavish, brightly-colored figures, often concealed within vegetation. These paintings, along with the "Fleurs, Fruits et Légumes" (Flowers, Fruits, and Vegetables) series developed in the 1980s, exhibit a masterful use of technique, and a complex exploration of social relations and the natural environment.

By that decade, Reyes had perfected a technique of painting and drawing using continuous curved lines. The characters' skin, as well as the fruits, vegetables, and plants, were created as if she were unraveling a long, thin thread across the surface. Colombian critic Álvaro Medina (*1941) described this technique: "To fill the figures, Emma Reyes' lines are arranged in parallel segments that undulate or remain straight, and sometimes rotate around themselves in vast spirals of intricate quality. Reyes does not seem to conceive of a plane as an area delimited on the outside by a contour, but as rows of lines in infinite succession."[2]

In the paintings of these two late series, the artist focused on depicting the countryside as a central figure, challenging the idea of urban spaces as epicenters of the world and embracing visions of rural futurity. Each character of the "Portraits Imaginaires" series is usually represented holding wild animals and fruits. Their shiny eyes convey emotion, and highlight that they are offering something vital to themselves, like a treasure, creating a poignant connection with the viewer. The rich vegetation in each painting evokes other artistic moments, such as the anthropomorphic portraits created by Italian Renaissance painter Giuseppe Arcimboldo (1526–1593), who used fruits, flowers, fish, and other elements to create human-like figures. The paintings also bring to mind the vibrant portraits and landscapes of Frida Kahlo (1907–1954), who was influenced by the post-revolutionary moment in Mexico that reevaluated art with Indigenous roots. Like Arcimboldo and Kahlo, Reyes presents the human body as part of a larger microcosm composed of multiple botanical and animal life forms.

This embracing of the rural in her work confronts the dominance of Western cultural values, and the race and class privileges associated with urban life, while subtly reclaiming the significance of peripheral locations, experiences, and visions. The artist was critical of how a Eurocentric and white-centered idea of modernity sustained unequal development dynamics across the world, impacting the formation and functioning of nation-states. "The bourgeoisie has not been able to govern [in Colombia], much less with those little children who attend the modern high school and take classes at Oxford and Harvard. You must have [experienced economic hardship], worked in everything, and smelled everything. I trust that one day a *Chocoano* [from Chocó, the Pacific Coast in Colombia], or [a person] from another place with less refinement but greater roots in the country, can [govern and] face the tremendous situation in Colombia with better success," said the artist in 1999.[3]

Reyes' paintings from the 1980s address racialized questions of uprootedness, belongingness, immigration, identity, and community, distancing themselves from modernism's white and masculine canon. It is worth noting that all the characters in this series have dark skin—brownish, blue, or olive-green. In some cases, the artist made explicit connections with social and political events, such as in *Omaira* (1985), which was created as an emotional response to the eruption of the Nevado del Ruiz volcano in November 1985. This eruption resulted in the complete burial of the town of Armero, an agricultural community in the Andean region of Colombia. One of the most heartbreaking photographs of this tragedy, which claimed the lives of over 25,000 people, was the portrait of Omaira Sánchez, a young girl who perished while trapped in the mud. In Reyes' painting, the girl is depicted on the right side of the image, covered by foliage, wearing an expression of anguish. Beside her is a flower with dozens of petals delicately cascading like an avalanche. In 1998 the artist donated the painting to the Museo de Arte de Pereira, located near the site of the disaster in Colombia, through the Fondo Cultural del Café de Manizales.

In 1988, as a natural extension of her "Fleurs, Fruits et Légumes" series, Reyes created her most ambitious large-scale piece: a fresco at the Bibliothèque Municipale de Périgueux, a small city in the region of Nouvelle-Aquitaine, southwestern France. The 14-meter mural depicts an agricultural landscape, including asparagus, onions, pears, radishes, celery, cauliflowers, and strawberries, while the extended roots across the painting resemble entanglements of long hair. The contrast between the scene represented and the place in which it is situated, suggests the garden is a library of another type.

By focusing on plants, these later works pay attention to regenerative practices, cultivation, and nurturing. Far from being a dull crop inventory, the paintings offer a vivid, sensual, and captivating exploration of organic forms. The artists pay attention to close-ups and details, as if capturing the flower's metabolic changes, or the interaction between plants and pollinators. The portrayal of vegetables serves as a specific form of political commentary, inviting us to think about our place in an increasingly urbanized world. Reyes depicts fruits and flowers as forces of change and living sources of knowledge that call for the repair of the relationship between people and nature.

1   See Emma Reyes, *The Book of Emma Reyes: A Memoir*, Penguin, London 2017.
2   Álvaro Medina, "Los cuarenta años de una linea," in *Emma Reyes y su pintura*, Excelsior Impresores, Bogotá, 1996, p. 11–12. My translation.
3   See Carlos-Enrique Ruiz, "Emma Reyes: mujer que respeta solo lo vivido," *Aleph*, no. 110, July/September 1999, Bogotá, p. 17–33. My translation.

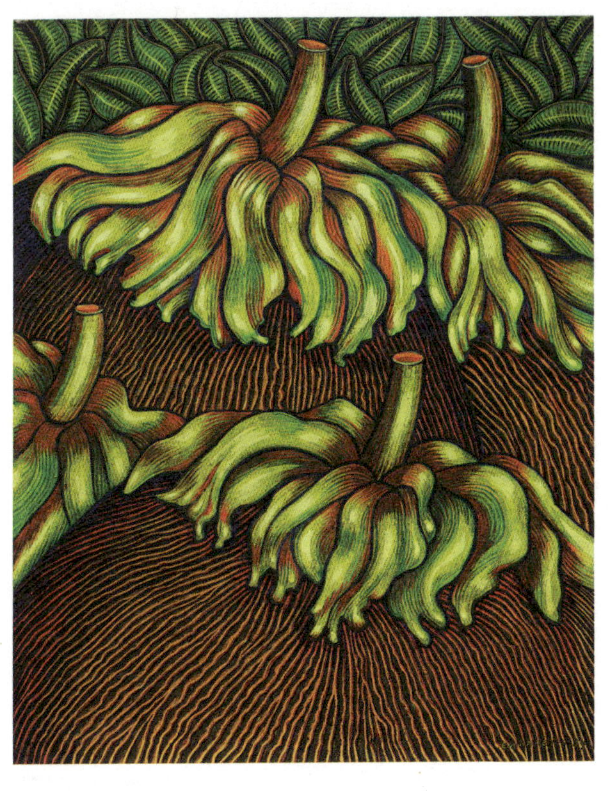

Untitled, 1984
Acrylic paint on canvas, 100 × 81 cm

[p. 13–27, 41]
"Flowers, Fruits and Vegetables" series, 1984–1993

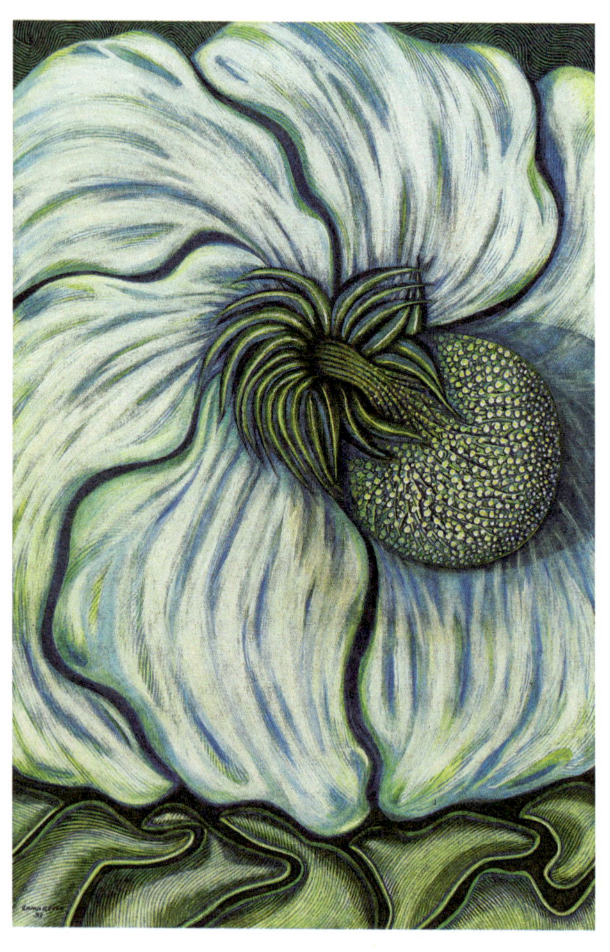

Untitled, 1993
Acrylic paint on canvas, 194 × 130 cm

14

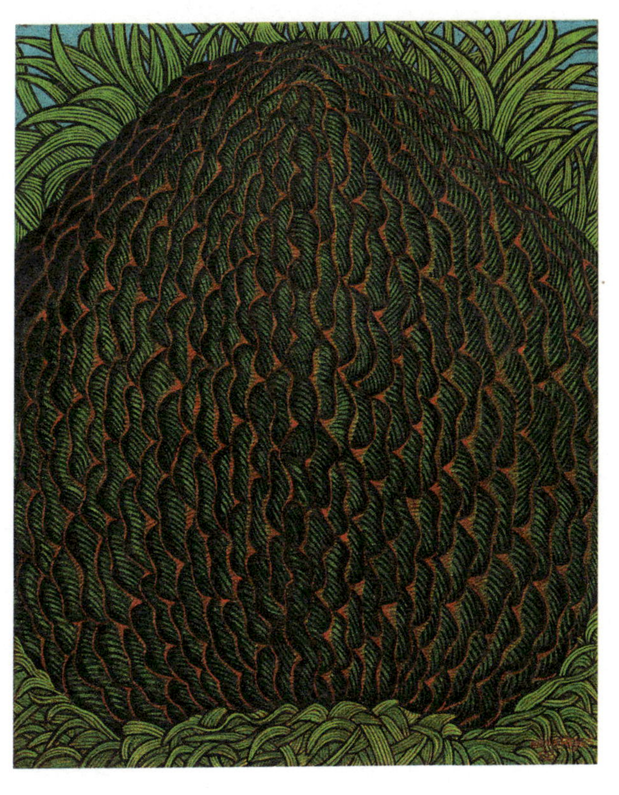

Untitled, 1988
Acrylic paint on canvas, 99 × 80.5 cm

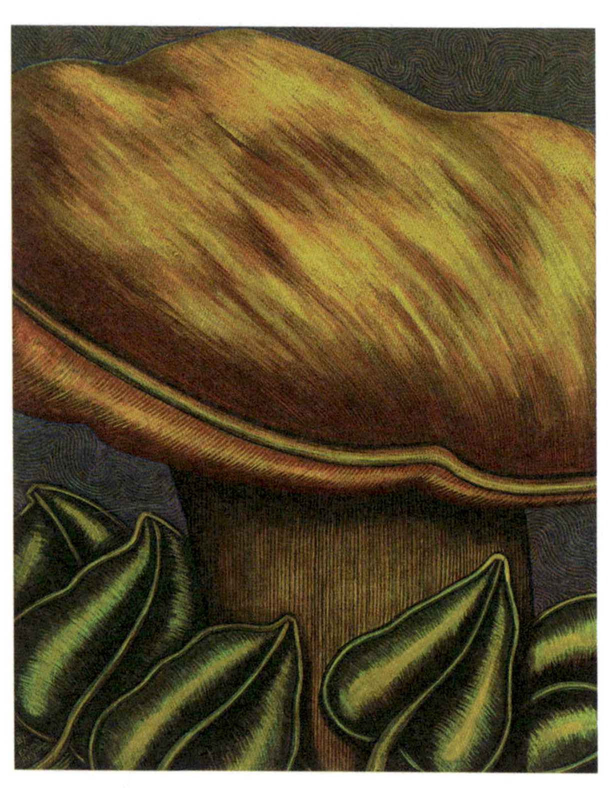

Untitled, 1987
Acrylic paint on canvas, 102 × 83 cm

16

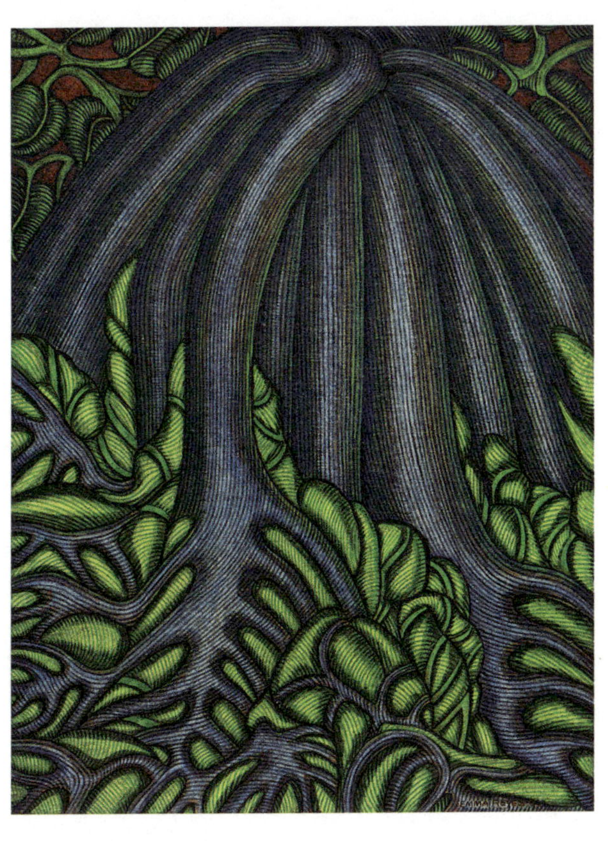

Untitled, 1988
Acrylic paint on canvas, 113 × 88 cm

"I abandoned the human figure to work with these flowers and vegetables. The forms have already been used in painting, but not as the sole subject of a picture, and always in the context of a still life, placed on a table or associated with other objects. The difference is that here they are the true and exclusive subject of the work. For this, direct and meticulous observation is necessary, an intimacy with the object, sometimes thanks to a magnifying glass—a familiarity with these organic beings which, when looked at carefully, are always a marvelous lesson in natural architecture. The result is single-entry paintings, generally no more than two planes, in which, like a landscape, you can wander among the stems, veins, and textures, explore the surfaces, caress the skin, and observe the horizons."

Emma Reyes, conversation with Camillo Calderón, *Magazín Aldia*, no. 99, April 5, 1993, Bogotá, p. 48

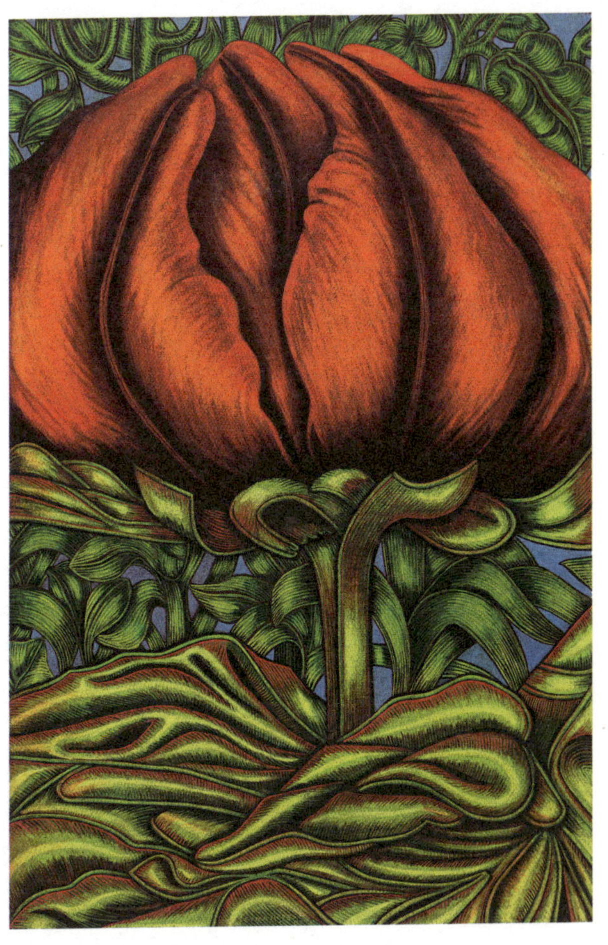

Untitled, 1980
Acrylic paint on canvas, 194 × 130 cm

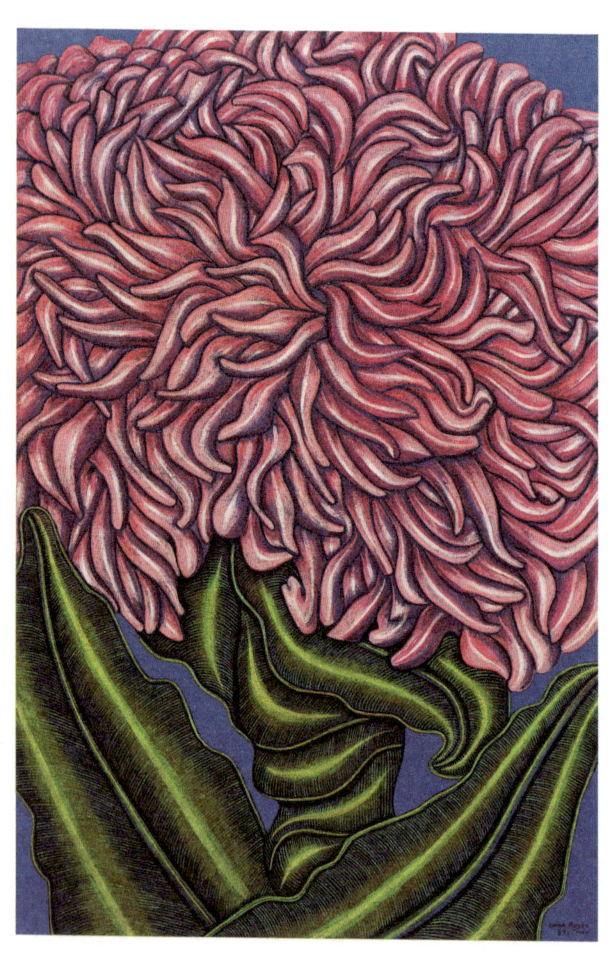

Untitled, 1989
Acrylic paint on canvas, 194 x 130 cm

20

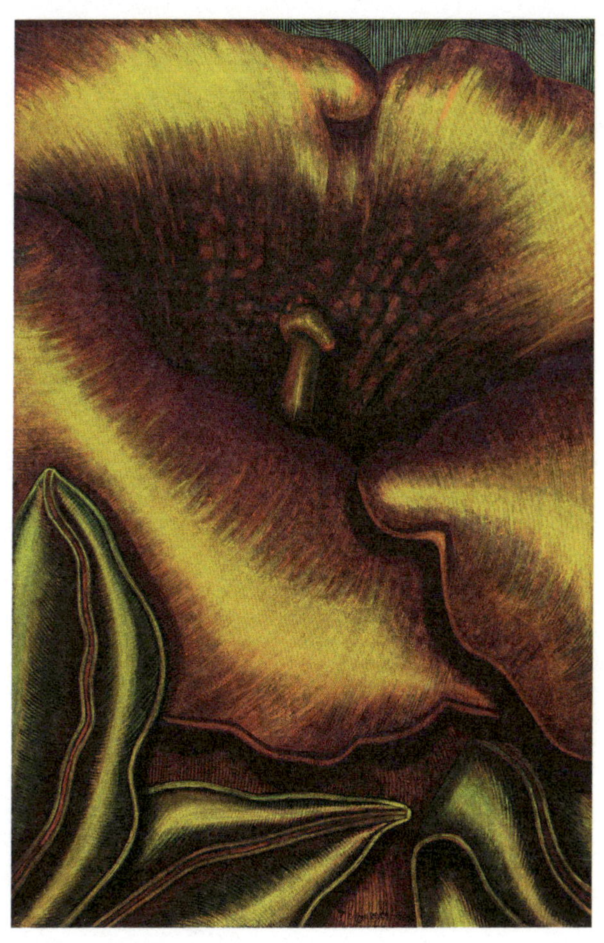

Untitled, 1992
Acrylic paint on canvas, 194 × 130 cm

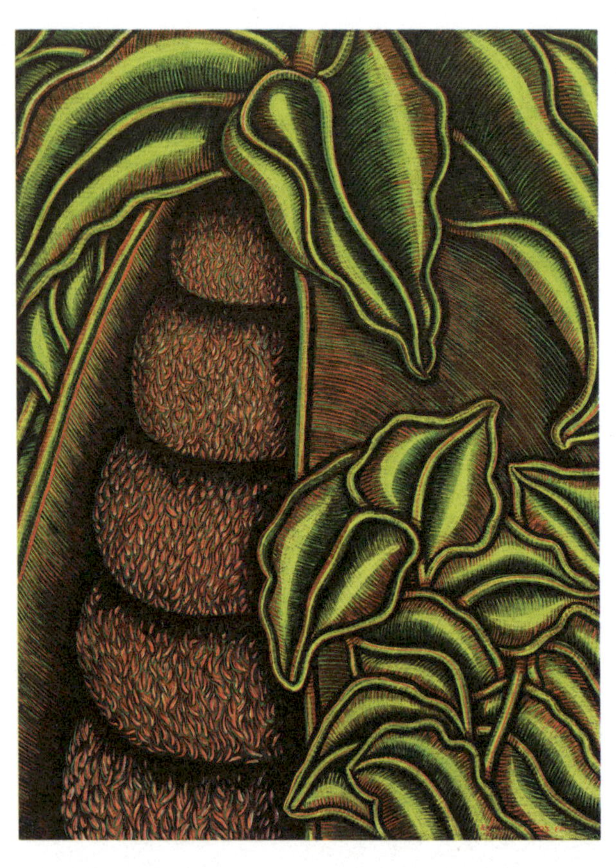

Untitled, 1987
Acrylic paint on canvas, 130 × 96 cm

22

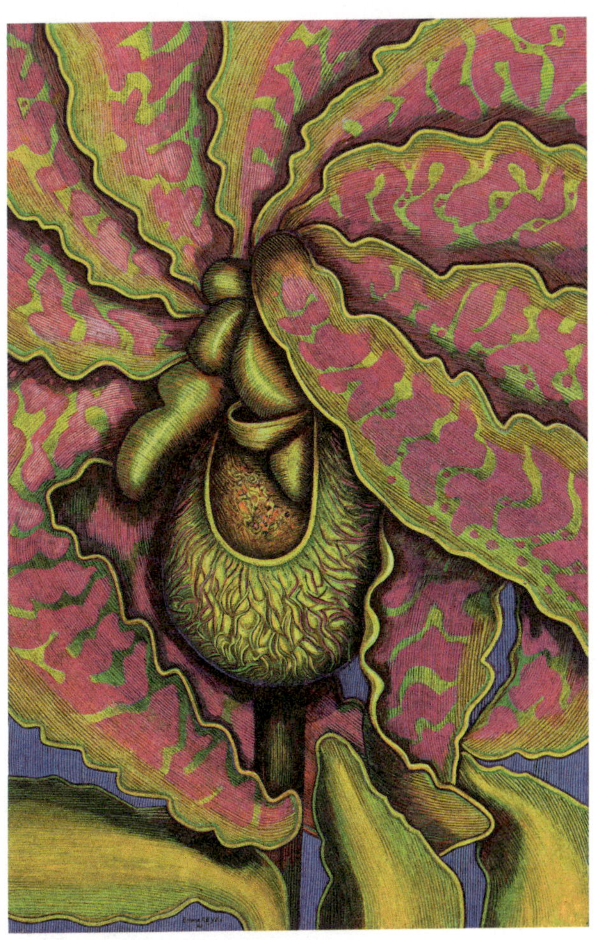

L'Orchidée anthropophage
(The Anthropophagous Orchid), 1990
Acrylic paint on canvas, 194 × 130 cm

"The important thing about my work is not whether it is good or bad, whether people like it or not, but that it has the authenticity of my geography. When people see it here in Europe, they immediately associate it with Latin America—the French exclaim: 'Amazonia!' My painting has the color, form, and baroque style of my roots."

Emma Reyes, conversation with Conchita Penilla-Céspedes, *Revista Diners*, no. 256, July 1991, Bogotá, p. 60

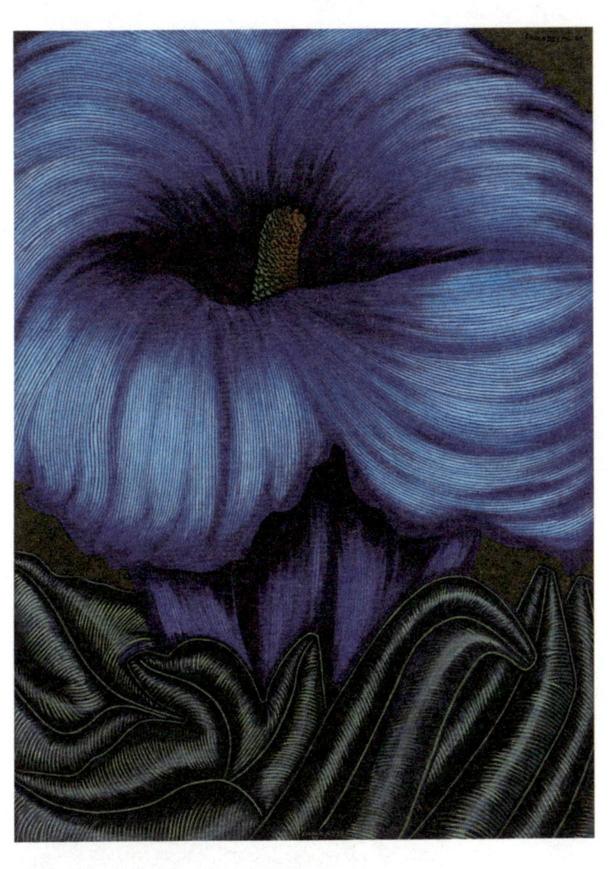

Untitled, 1988–1989
Acrylic paint on canvas, 130 × 96 cm

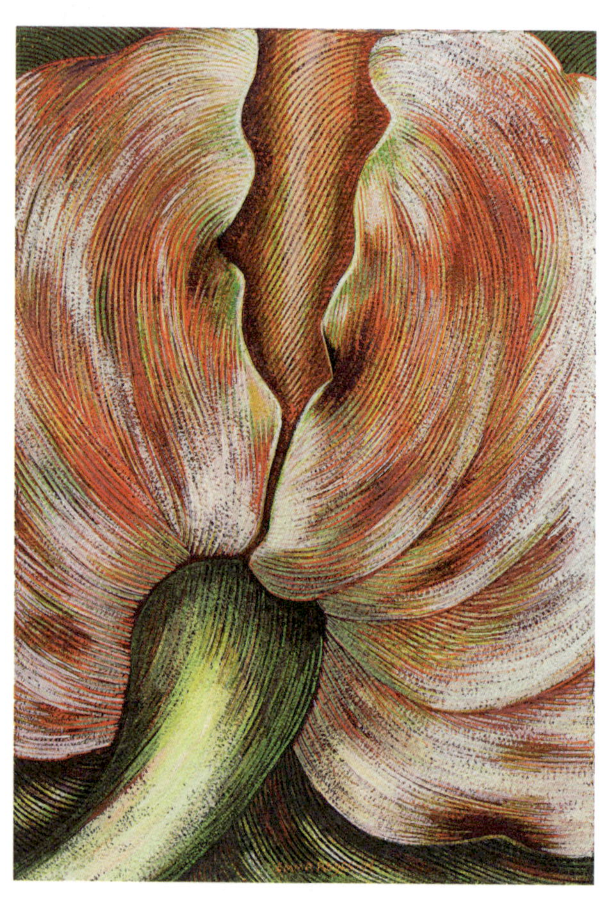

Untitled, 1991
Acrylic paint on paper, 133 × 83 cm

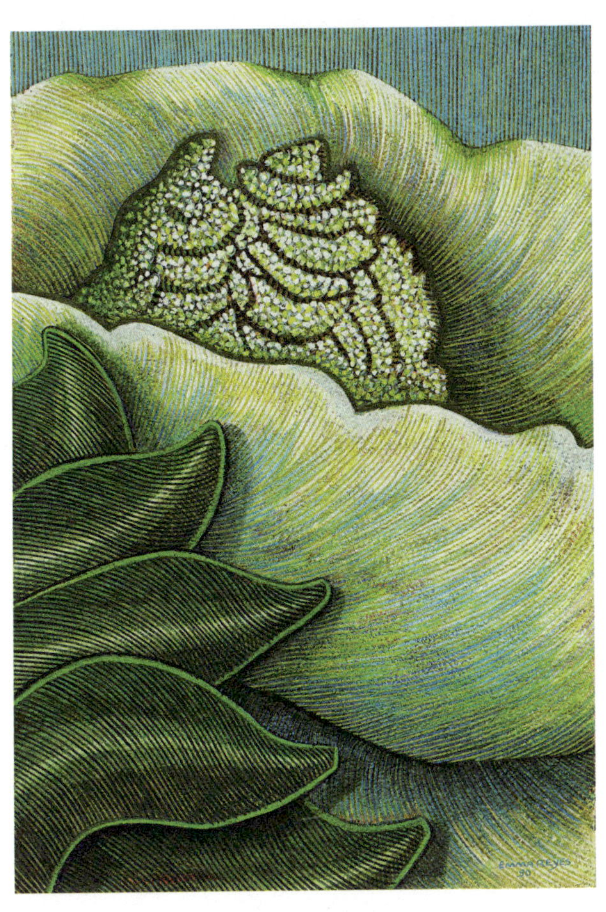

Untitled, 1990
Acrylic paint on paper, 133 × 83 cm

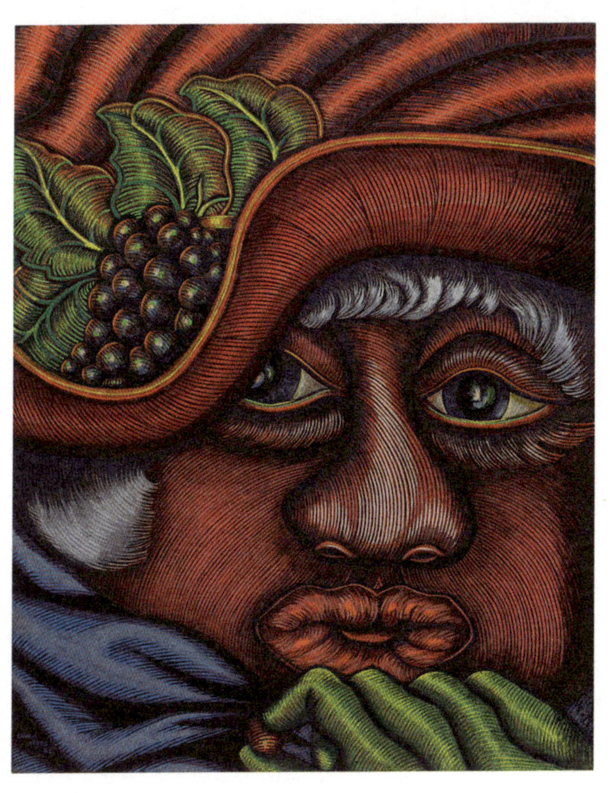

Untitled, 1985
Acrylic paint on canvas, 100 × 80.5 cm

[p. 1, 4, 29–35]
"Imaginary Portraits" series, 1985–1990

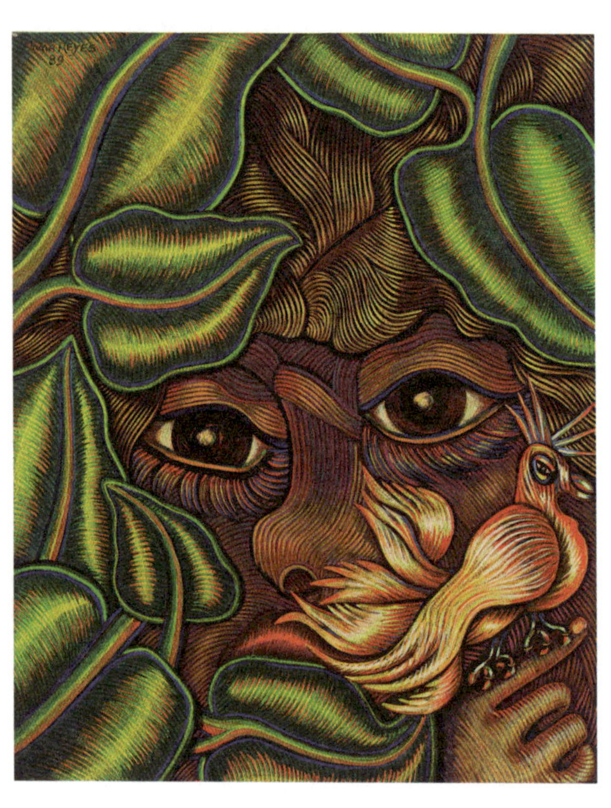

Untitled, 1989
Acrylic paint on canvas, 100 × 80.5 cm

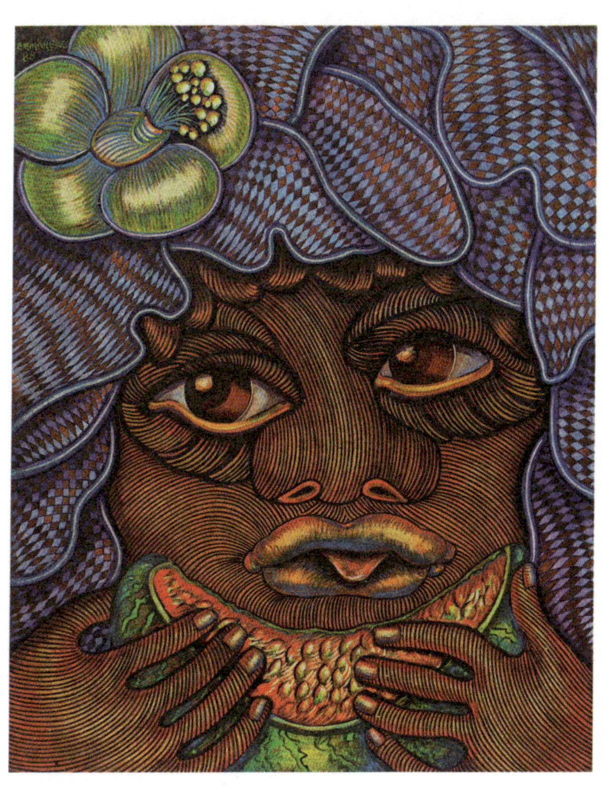

Untitled, 1988
Acrylic paint on canvas, 100 × 96 cm

"Painting should be an act of sincerity. I have lived in Europe for 40 years and, despite everything, people realize that I'm different. Something similar has to happen to my painting. I keep telling the young painters from South America this: we have to create our own culture. We have to put an end to this colonial attitude toward our own culture."

Emma Reyes, conversation with José Hernandez, *Américas*, June–July 1986, Paris, p. 10

Untitled, 1991
Acrylic paint on canvas, 130 × 73 cm

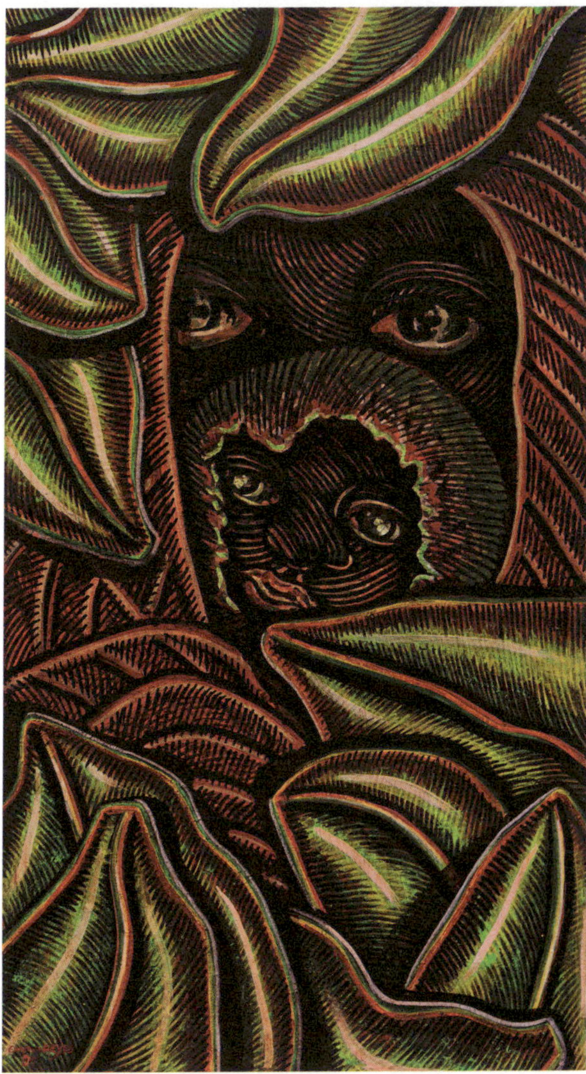

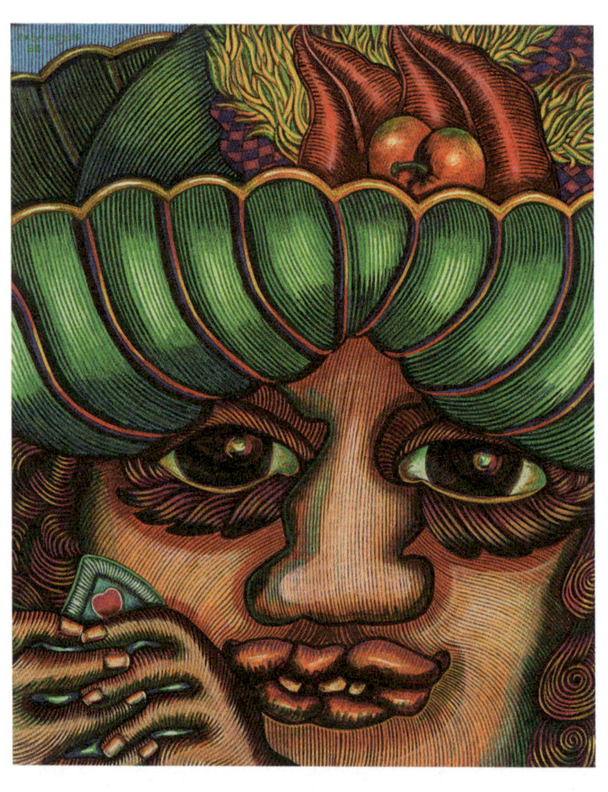

Untitled, 1990
Acrylic paint on canvas, 100 × 80.5 cm

34

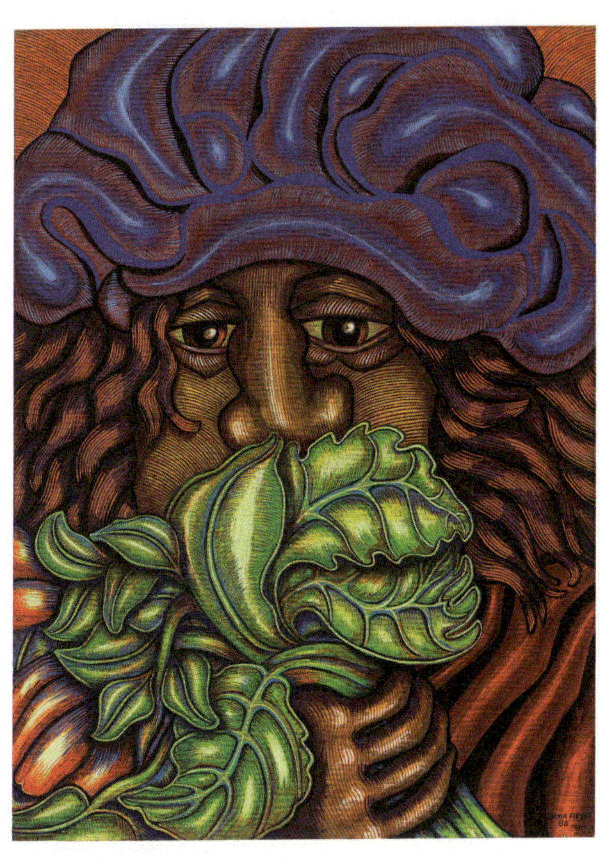

Untitled, 1985
Acrylic paint on canvas, 130 × 96.50 cm

Natureculture According to Emma Reyes

Stéphanie Cottin

Colombian artist Emma Reyes was a self-taught painter. She did, however, spend time studying and working under the French and Mexican artists André Lhote (1885–1962) and Diego Rivera (1886–1957), from whom she learned an important life lesson: to stay true to what made both her work and her background undeniably unique.

The term "magic realism," which describes a trend in late 20th-century Latin-American literary fiction represented by, among others, Miguel Ángel Asturias, Carlos Fuentes, and Gabriel García Márquez, could equally be applied to Reyes' body of work. In the mid-1950s, she began portraying "Monstres" (Monsters)—part-human, part-animal hybrids—in her paintings, taking cues from Italian artist Enrico Prampolini (1894–1956), and adopting a formal vocabulary that combined elements of post-Cubist and pre-Columbian art. This "animistic" tendency would remain central to her work from this point on. Some Andean animist societies see weaving and embroidery as a way of bringing the object of representation to life. Reyes perpetuated this approach in her own fashion: using oft-recurring thread and ring patterns, she instilled in her subjects an animated quality. Far from being fixed, her paintings are infused with organic energy, like moving images on a TV screen.

Reyes roundly rejected the expression "still life," pushing back against the singularly Western and hierarchical manner of representing the world materially and objectively. Instead, she sought to understand humans in their biological and social environment, and not merely in the company of other humans. Reyes was acutely aware that people have never been alone in the world: we have always interacted with other species, both animals and plants, and our story is one built on collaboration and shared progress. Drawing not on scientific fact but on the imagination, she used her paintings to tell stories of socialization between species. And in doing so she emphasized how, as Belgian philosopher Vinciane Despret puts it, we owe a "debt" to those "with whom we have become what we are today."[1]

This publication brings together a selection of Reyes' paintings from the 1980s and early 1990s. This was the period when the artist departed furthest from Western ideas and adopted a distinctively South American world-view in her work, after flirting briefly—during her time in Rome and Paris—with contemporary "isms": post-Cubism, Abstract Expressionism, Nouveau Réalisme, and Kinetic art.

Her early series of "Portraits Imaginaires" (Imaginary Portraits), which appear to be woven in black and white from a kind of primordial mate-rial, gave rise, in the late 1970s, to a more flam-boyant period in which she drew on her identity, on memories of her journey across Latin America in the early 1940s, and on her time spent in the Paraguayan jungle. Each brightly colored can-vas features the same spidery lines that became a hallmark of her work. In her paintings, Reyes depicted individuals set among lush vegetation: the human being and the surrounding jungle are as one. In portraying her subjects alongside animals, or with a piece of fruit in their arms or raised to their lips, she sought to tell an ancient story of kinship. But far from calling for a return to the wild, Reyes rejected the anthropocentric worldview and hoped to return humanity to its rightful place, in dialogue with its environment.

Reyes also produced close-up paintings of flowers, fruits, and vegetables, portraying them as living beings in the series "Fleurs, Fruits et Légumes" (Flowers, Fruits, and Vegetables). Through her systematic use of tightly framed composition, she endeavored to transform our relationship with the physical world, to bring us closer to nature. Like Georgia O'Keeffe (1887–1986), she forces the viewer to focus intently on the subject. Reyes' approach—masterful portraits of fruits and flowers that push beyond the confines of deliberately undersized frames—set her apart from the formal concerns of her contemporaries, but allowed her to reconnect with the full and complete expression of her cultural identity.

In 1988, Reyes produced a fresco for the Bibliothèque Municipale de Périgueux in France. In its scale and subject—14 meters long and featuring brightly colored flowers—it gives the impression of dominating the observer. By installing larger-than-life plants in a public place of knowledge and learning, the artist seems to suggest that culture and nature are not opposites, but two sides of the same coin. In this sense, Reyes' art bears similarities to the concept of "natureculture" proposed by American scholar Donna Haraway.[2] By reversing the roles in this way (the plant observing the visitor), Reyes questions the notion that humanity is the exclusive writer of the story of nature.

Through her creations, she made an important contribution to the debate around modern anthropocentrism and Eurocentrism in art. Reyes' body of work has presaged this paradigm shift, imploring us to rethink our view of the world and our place in it.

1	Vinciane Despret, foreword, in Donna Haraway, *Manifeste des espèces compagnes. Chiens, humains et autres partenaires*, Flammarion, Paris 2018, p. 18.
2	See Donna Haraway, *The Companion Species Manifesto: Dogs, People, and Significant Otherness*, Prickly Paradigm Press, Chicago 2003.

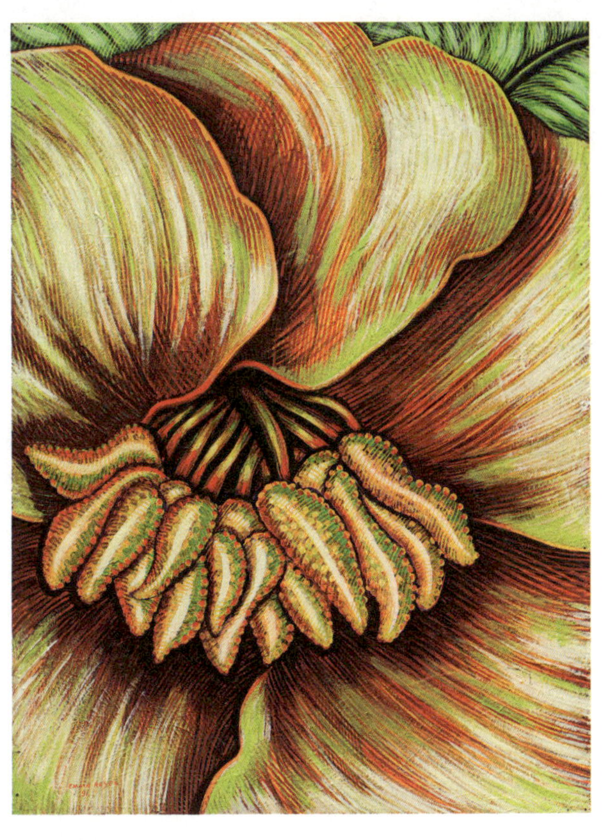

Untitled, 1991
Acrylic paint on paper on plywood, 125.5 × 96 cm

→

Emma Reyes in her studio, Rome, c. 1956

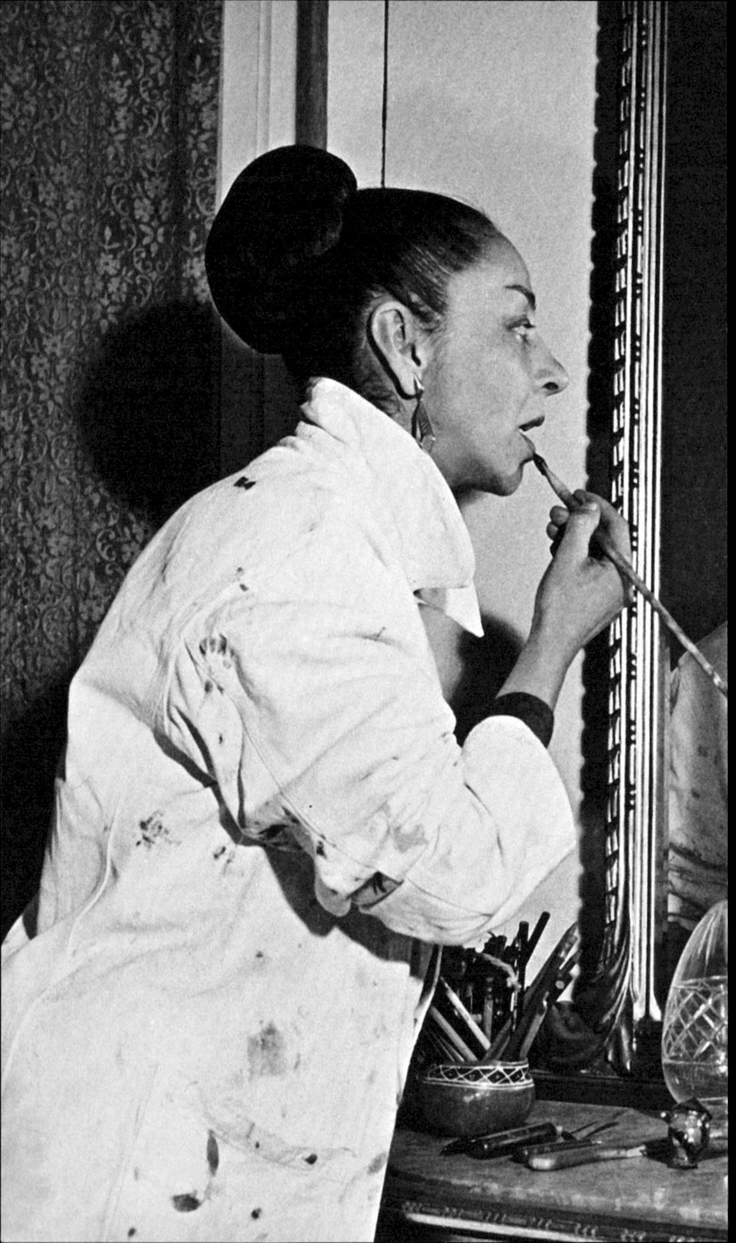

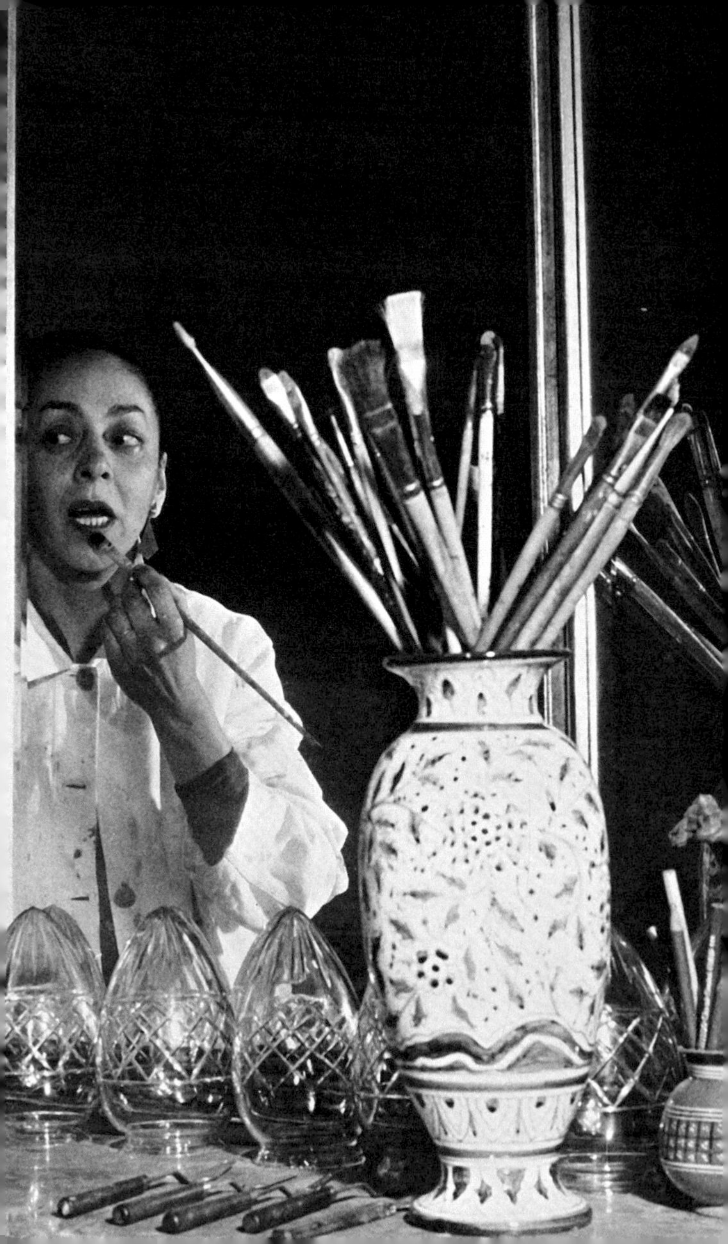

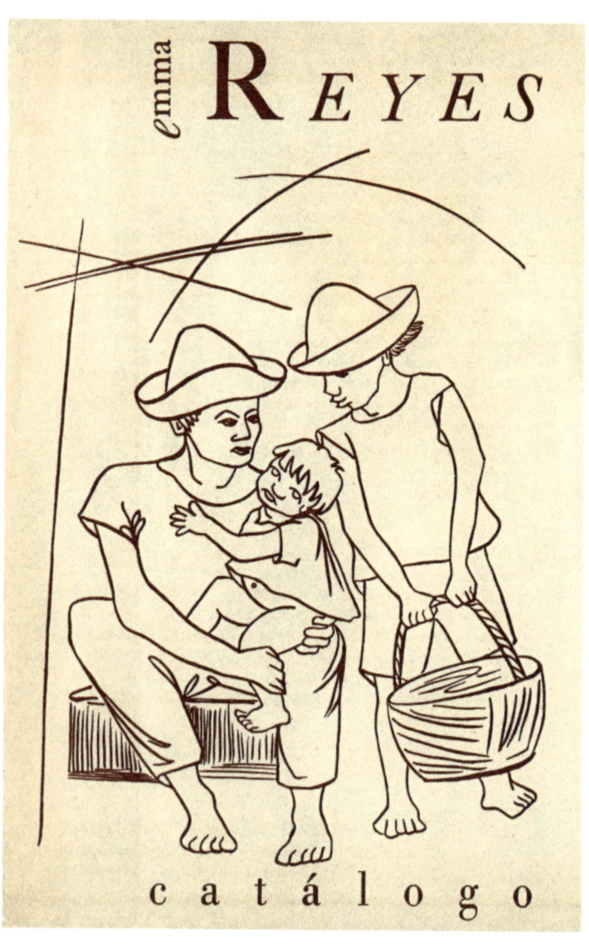

Cover of the booklet for Emma Reyes solo exhibition
at the Galería Arte Contemporáneo of Lola Álvarez Bravo,
Mexico City, 1952

Emma Reyes' Biography
Bogotá, 1919–Bordeaux, 2003

Born illegitimate in 1919, Emma Reyes was abandoned at the age of five by her mother on a
railway platform, and placed with her older
sister Helena in the convent of the Auxiliary
Sisters of Bogotá, from where she fled at the
age of 18 in 1937. In 1940, she decided to leave
Colombia and travelled around Latin America
doing a multitude of odd jobs. She settled in
Buenos Aires in 1943. Self-taught, she began
painting at the end of 1945, after discovering
an exhibition by Argentine painter Raúl Soldi
(1905–1994) at the Salón Peuser. It was the first
time she had seen paintings and entered a
gallery. She immediately produced her first
water-colors, her "first naive paintings" as she
described them in 1964. She moved to Montevideo,
Uruguay, and subsequently to Caacupé, Paraguay.
Her stay in the Paraguayan jungle in 1946–1947
left a lasting impression on her, and determined
her vocation. In the spring of 1947, she fled the
violence of the Paraguayan civil war to return
to Buenos Aires, where she became close to the
Argentine painter Antonio Berni (1905–1981) and
obtained a Fondation Roncoroni scholarship to

study at the Académie André Lhote in Paris. On the transatlantic liner to Le Havre, she met the painter Alejo Vidal-Quadras (1919–1994) and the physician Jean Perromat (1915–2006), who became her husband in 1962.

In 1949, she held her first solo exhibition in Paris, at the Galerie Kléber. Her works, which could be described as "primitive," focused on the human figure, evoking the Mexican Muralists, whose work she was not yet familiar with, and who she had not yet met. In 1950, Reyes was invited to Washington by the Division of Education of the Pan American Union, under the aegis of UNESCO, to illustrate literacy publications for the Latin American People's Library for a two-year period. She moved to Mexico City in 1952 where she worked in the studio of Diego Rivera (1886–1957), and assisted photographer Lola Álvarez Bravo (1903–1993) at her Galería Arte Contemporáneo, where she had a solo exhibition. She also took part in the 8th Pan American Congress of Architects. She was appointed as a designer at the School and Foreign Theater section of Mexico City's National Institute of Fine Arts. She resigned at the end of 1953 and left Mexico.

Reyes moved to Italy in 1954, where she became the collaborator and final companion of artist Enrico Prampolini (1894–1956). Through her contact with him, she developed her "Monsters" series and explored the relationship between abstraction, figuration, and geometry. In 1957, the Institute for Cultural Relations between Israel and Latin America invited her to stay in the village and artists' colony Ein Hod in Israel. Impressed by the natural world she found there, she painted her first and only landscapes. From 1958 to 1960, she returned to Italy.

Reyes moved permanently to France in 1960, where she lived between Paris and Périgueux until 1990, and then in Bordeaux until her death in 2003. At the time, she was one of the central figures of the Latin American artistic and cultural scene in Paris, and was affectionately nicknamed "Mama Grande." She made five journeys to Colombia between 1960 and 1990 to work on artistic projects. In France, working between nativism, animism, and Magic Realism, she sought to reappropriate the forms of her own culture through various European artistic developments, and to propose a non-Western style—without perspective, derived from her years of embroidery learned in the convent, Colombian basketry, and the artifacts of pre-Columbian cultures—the better to ani-mate, decolonize, and tropicalize easel painting, the Western medium par excellence. "We have to create our own culture. We have to put an end to this colonial attitude toward our own culture," she asserted in the monthly magazine *Américas* in 1986. She was named Chevalier des Arts et des Lettres in 1996. From 1998 onward, Reyes, exhausted, could hardly paint at all, and concentrated on writing.

A collection of letters sent between 1969 and 1997 to her lifelong friend, Colombian diplomat, historian, and journalist Germán Arciniegas (1900–1999)—who she met on December 10, 1948, the day UNESCO adopted the Universal Declaration of Human Rights, in the elevator of its Paris offices—was published in Colombia in 2012 under the title *Memoria por correspondencia*, later translated into French and English in 2017. Reyes did not consider herself a writer. Nevertheless, encouraged by Germán Arciniegas, Gabriel García Márquez, and Carlos-Enrique Ruiz, editor-in-chief of *Aleph*, she wrote for this Colombian cultural magazine. Her talent for storytelling came to the fore in her letters, which she hoped would be published posthumously.

This biography was compiled by Stéphanie Cottin based on current research and available information.

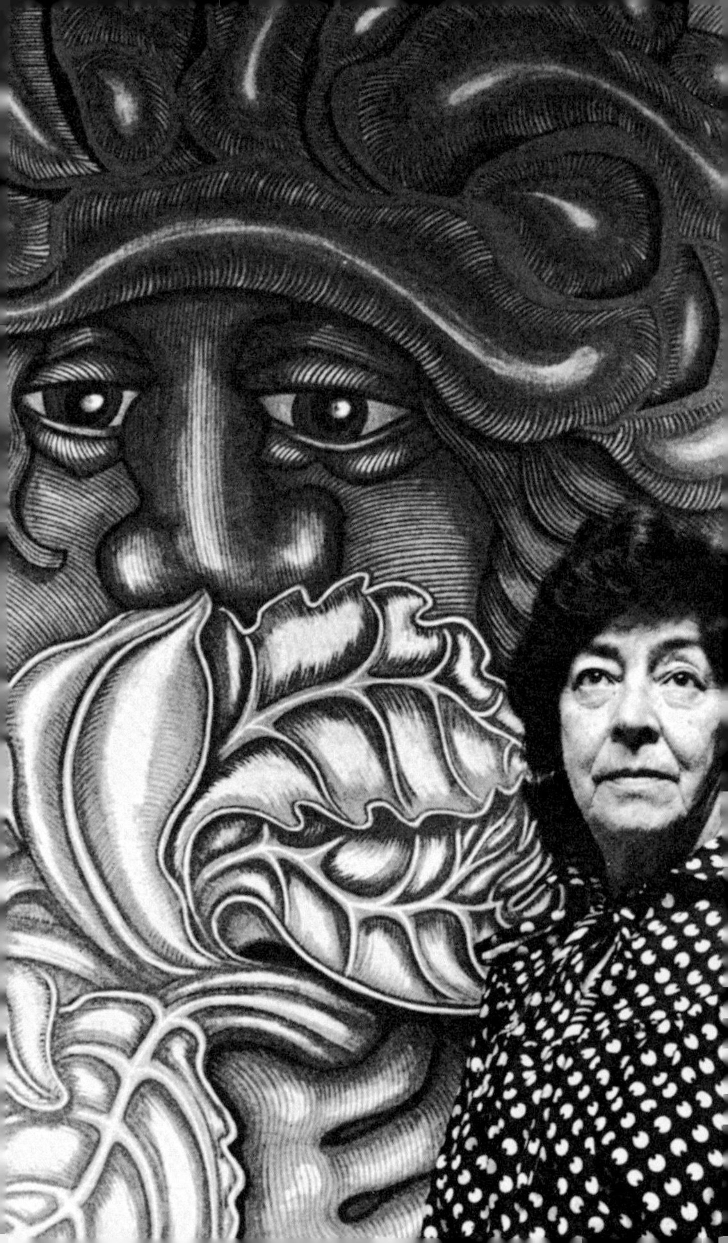

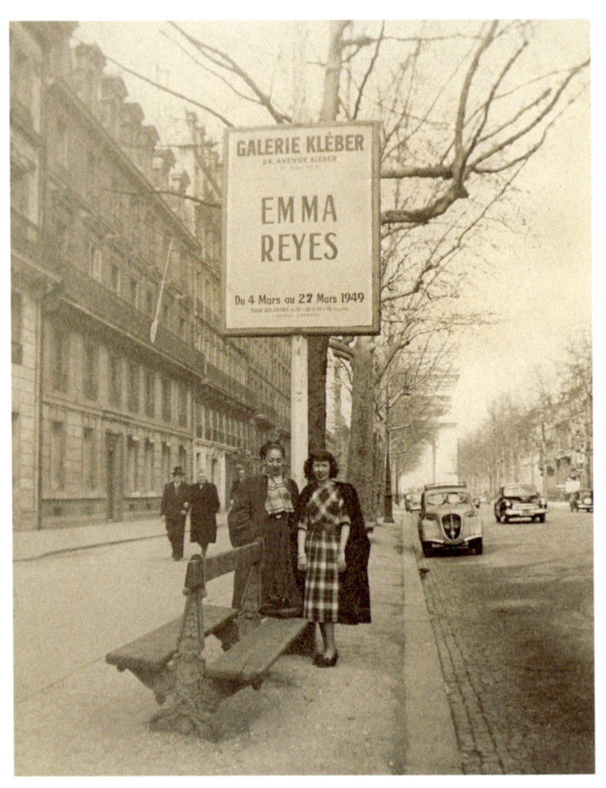

Emma Reyes and Beatriz Piedrahita, Paris, 1949

←

Emma Reyes in her studio in front of one of her
"Imaginary Portraits," Paris, c. 1980

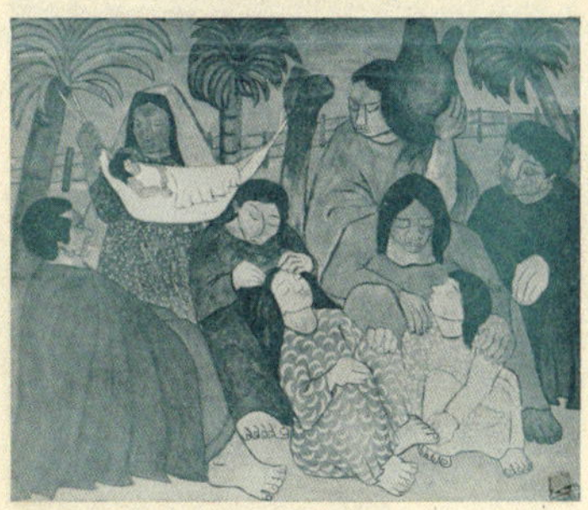

Poster for Emma Reyes' first solo exhibition (54 artworks), Galerie Kléber, Paris, 1949

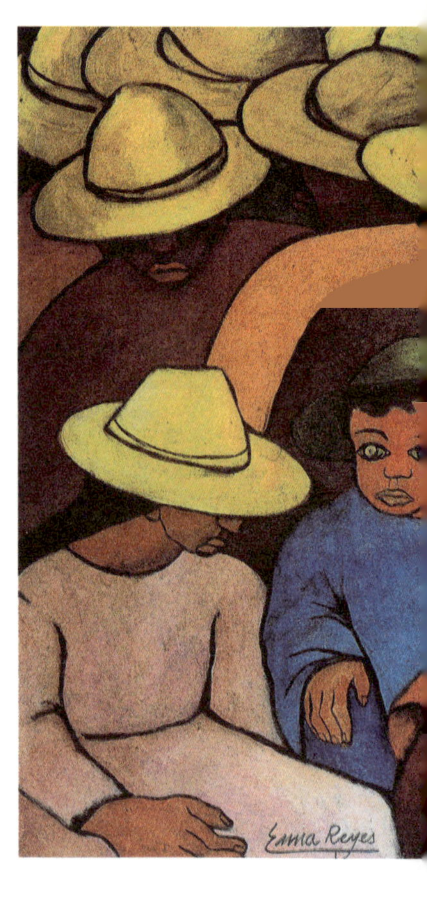

Untitled, 1948
Oil on paper, 98.5 x 73 cm

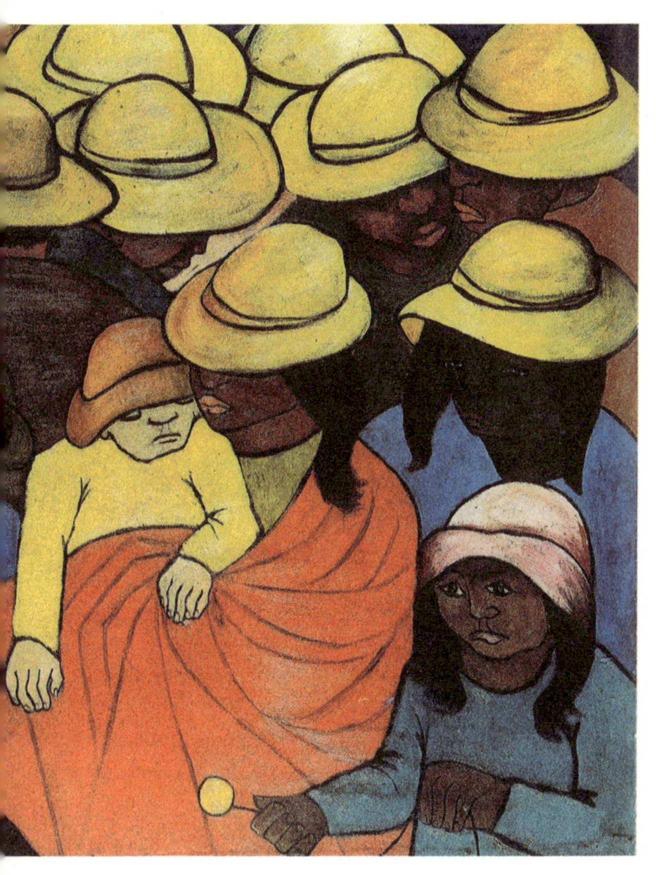

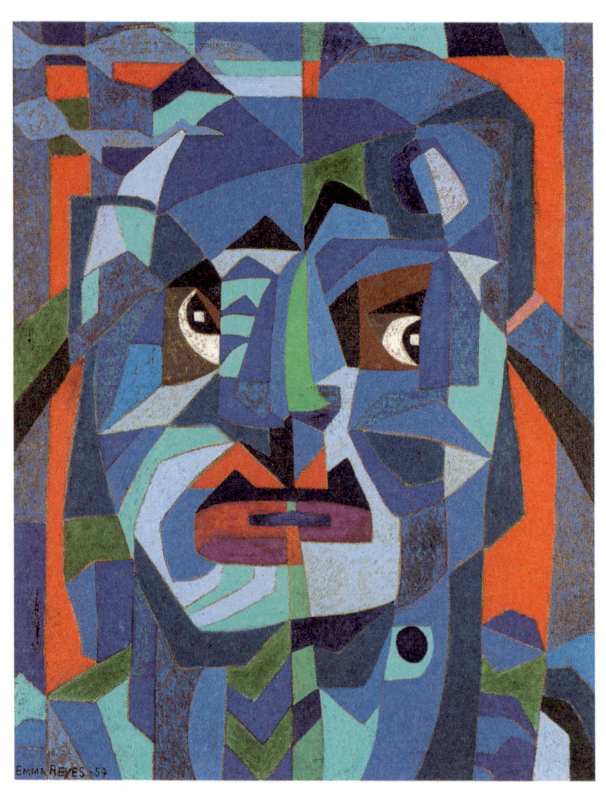

Portrait of Moravia, "Monsters" series, 1957
Oil on canvas, 100 × 81 cm

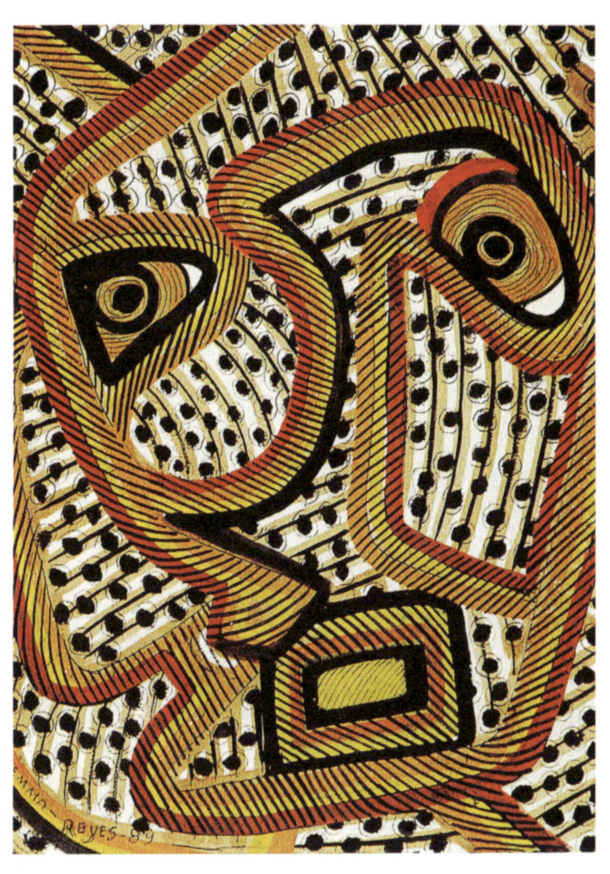

Mask, 1989
Acrylic on paper, 41 x 31 cm

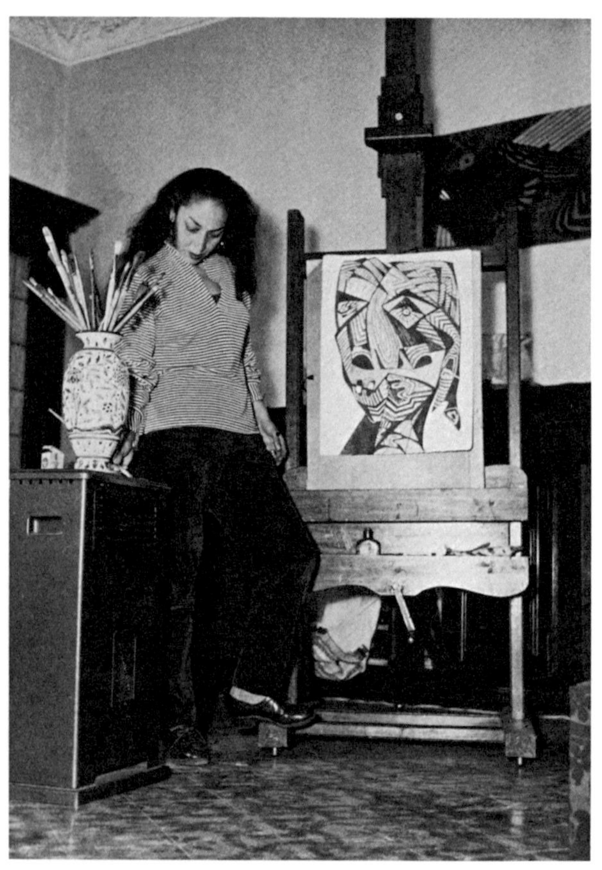

Emma Reyes in her studio located on the via Eleonora Duse,
Rome, c. 1954–1956
A work from the "Monsters" series is on the easel
that was given to her by her Argentinian friends upon
her departure in 1947

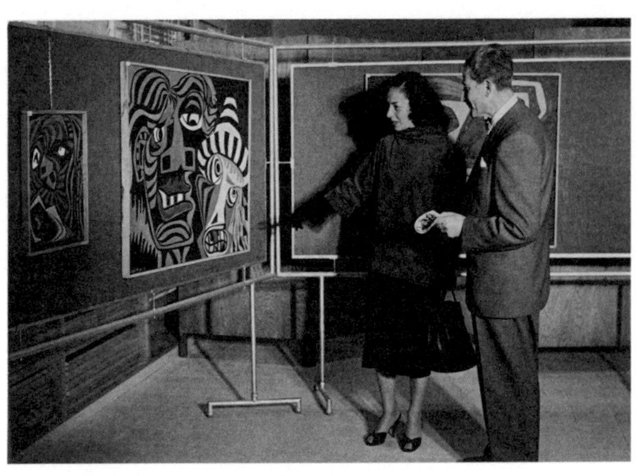

Emma Reyes at the opening of the solo exhibition
at ZOA House, Tel Aviv, 1958

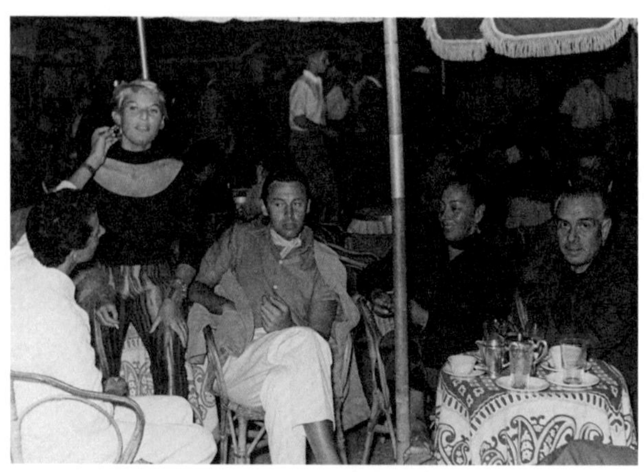

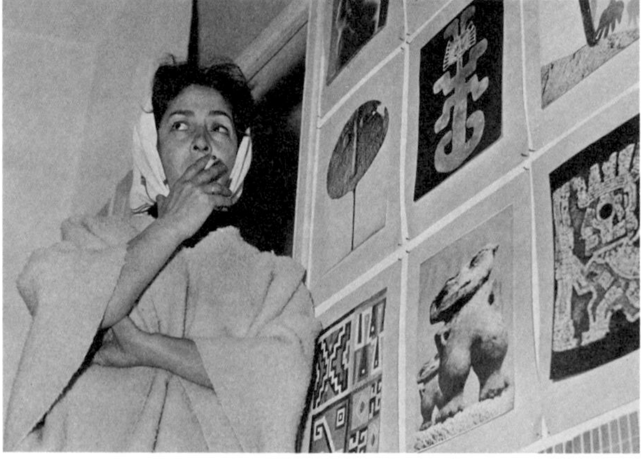

Tilda Thamar, Alejo Vidal-Quadras, Emma Reyes, and Enrico Prampolini, Capri, 1954

Emma Reyes in her Roman studio in front of a wall featuring photographs of pre-Colombian artifacts, c. 1957–1960

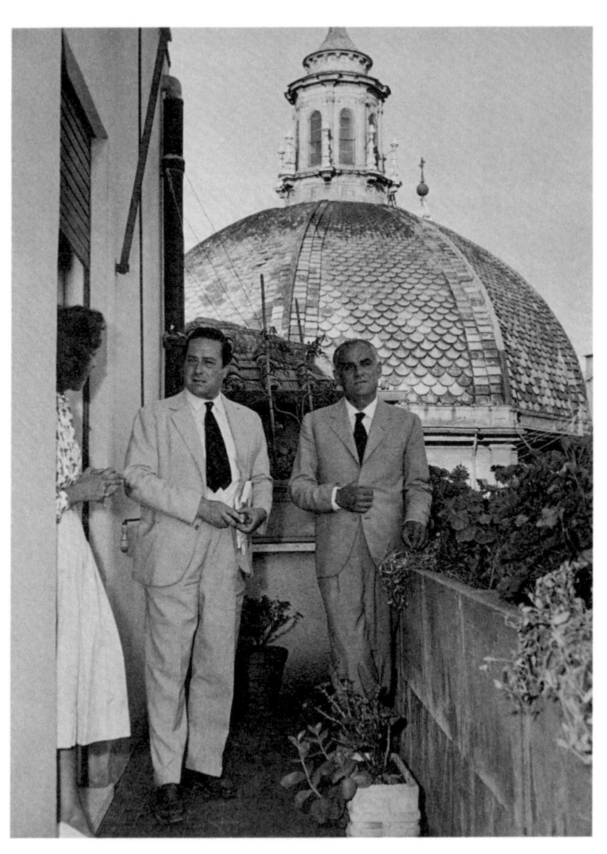

Emma Reyes, Alberto Moravia, and Abelardo Arias, on
the balcony of Alberto Moravia's apartment, via dell'Oca,
Rome, 1957

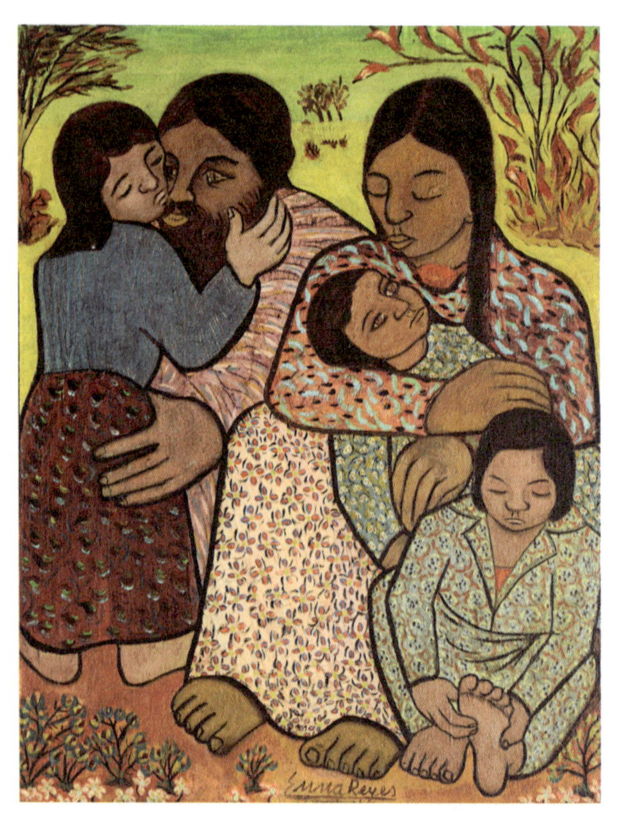

Untitled, c. 1940
Oil on canvas, 70 x 55 cm

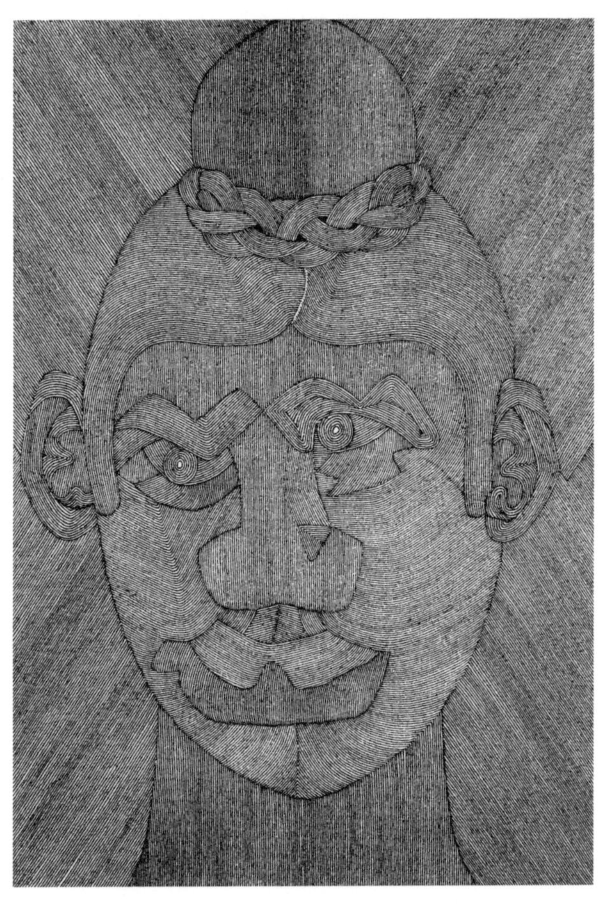

Work from Emma Reyes' first black-and-white "Imaginary
Portraits" series, 1970s

Solo Exhibitions

1949   Galerie Kléber, Paris

1952   Galería Arte Contemporáneo, Mexico City

1954   Wall fresco for the main hall of the transatlantic
       liner Cavelier-de-la-Salle
       Wall fresco for the villa La Lampara, Capri

1956   Galleria delle Carrozze, Rome
       Galleria Monte Napoleone, Milan

1958   Bezalel National Museum, Jerusalem
       ZOA House, Tel Aviv Museum, Tel Aviv
       Museum of Modern Art, Haifa
       Ein Hod Art Gallery, Ein Hod

1959   Galleria Schneider, Rome

1960   Galleria Monte Napoleone, Milan

1961   Galería El Callejón, Bogotá
       Museo de Arte Moderno La Tertulia, Cali

1963   Galerie Vendôme, Brussels

1965   Dugith Art Gallery, Tel Aviv

1966   Decoration for the École Normale, Périgueux

1967   Galerie de Beaune, Paris

1968   Galeria Botto, Caracas
       Biblioteca Luis Ángel Arango, Banco de la República,
       Bogotá
       Museo de Zea (Museo de Antioquia), Medellin
       Museo de Arte Moderno La Tertulia, Cali
       Galería Lirolay, Buenos Aires

1973   Galerie Les Trois Portes, Mons
       Sara Gilat Gallery, Jerusalem

1974   Galerie L'Atelier, Brussels

1975   Galería Ciento, Barcelona
       Galerie H et Multiples, Marseille

1976   Galería Esede, Bogotá

1983   Galerie Duszka Patÿn-Karolczak, Brussels

1983   Galería Garcez-Velasquez, Bogotá
        Museo de Arte Moderno La Tertulia, Cali
1985   Decoration for the Lycée Pablo-Picasso, Périgueux
1988   Wall fresco for the hall of the Bibliothèque
        Municipale de Périgueux, Périgueux
1990   Retrospective exhibition *Regard sur la peinture
        d'Emma Reyes,* Musée d'art et d'archéologie du
        Périgord–MAAP, Centre des Congrès, Chambre de
        Commerce et d'Industrie, Bibliothèque Municipale,
        Périgueux
1991   Galerie Richard Treger, Paris
1993   Museo de Arte Moderno La Tertulia, Cali
        Museo Rayo, Roldanillo
        Galería Diners, Bogotá
        Semaine de l'Amérique Latine, Pessac
2017   *Emma Reyes, peintre*, Musée d'art et d'archéologie
        du Périgord–MAAP, Périgueux
2022   *Emma Reyes peintre colombienne*, Maison des Arts,
        Antony
2023   *Emma Reyes*, MAMCO, Geneva
2024   *Las Caras de Emma Reyes*, Galería La Cometa,
        Bogotá
2025   *Emma Reyes*, CAPC, Bordeaux

→

Partial view of the 14-meter-long fresco created in 1988 by
Emma Reyes for the Bibliothèque Municipale de Périgueux,
now the Bibliothèque Municipale Pierre-Fanlac

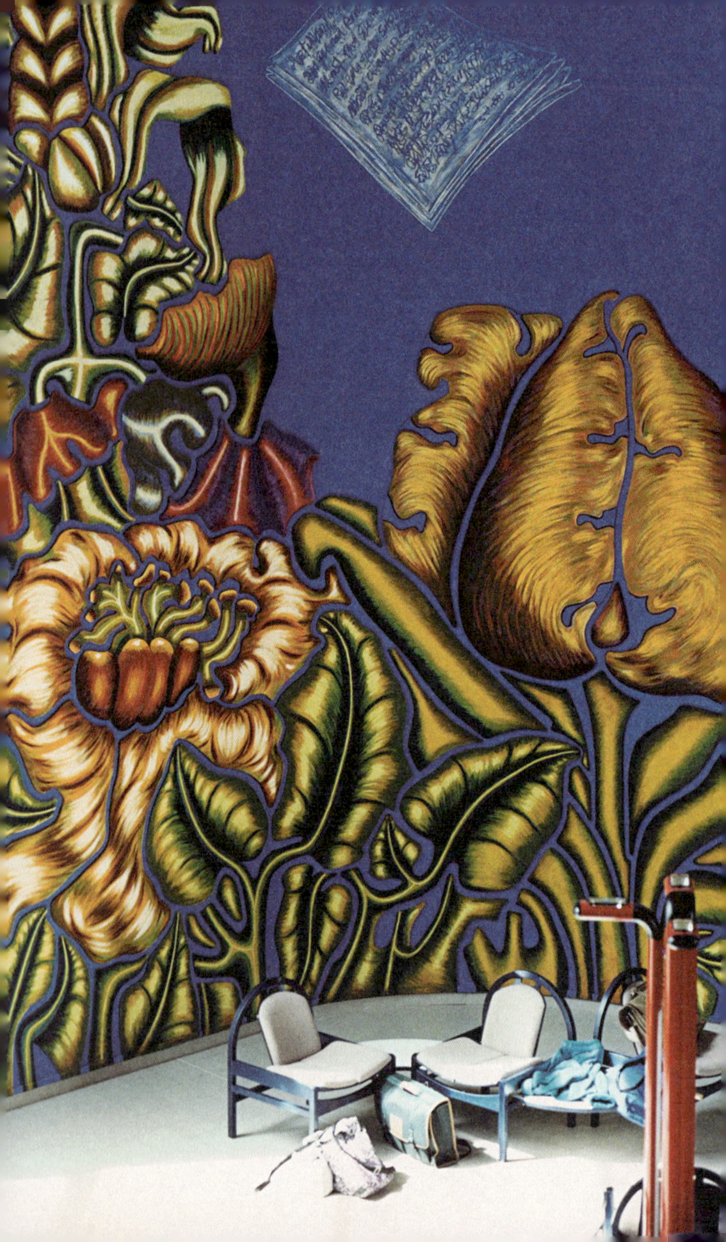

Major Group Exhibitions

1950   Dupont Gallery, White Gallery, F.A.I., Washington

1951   Martignon Gallery, New York
Lateinamerikanische Kunst der Gegenwart, touring
exhibition organized by the Pan American Union,
West Germany

1952   *Pintura y Grabado, XVIIe anniversario de la
Revolucion Mexicana*, Teatro Calderón, Zacatecas;
curated by Lola Álvarez Bravo, artworks by the
Mexican Muralists

1953   Morse Gallery of Art, Miami

1954   IVe Premio internazionale per le pittrici, Bolzano

1955   *Prima mostra d'arte interplanetaria*, Centro delle
arti Quo Vadis, Rome

1956   Galleria internazionale d'Arte moderna, Ca' Pesaro,
28th Venice Biennale, Venice

1959   *La Donna nell'arte contemporánea*, Galleria d'arte
Breda, Milan

1960   Ve Exposition internationale, organized by the Club
international féminin, Musée d'art moderne de la
Ville de Paris, Paris

1964   *Primitifs d'aujourd'hui*, Galerie Charpentier, Paris

1966   Salon des Beaux-Arts, Périgueux

1968   Ateneo, Madrid
VIIIe Festival de Arte, Cali

1970   Instituto Italo-Latinoamericano, Rome

1973   Bienal Americana de Artes Gráficas, Cali

1976   Bienal Americana de Artes Gráficas, Cali
Galerie Kaspari, Meerbusch

1979   Aberbach Fine Art, London

1980   *La Mujer en las artes visuales*, Museo de Arte
Moderno La Tertulia, Cali

1981   Bienal Americana de Artes Gráficas, Cali

1982   Art Basel, Galerie Rolf Kallenbach (Munich), Basel
        L'Amérique latine à Paris, Grand Palais, Paris
1998   Galerie des Beaux-Arts, Bordeaux
2024   *Stranieri ovunque. Foreigners Everywhere*,
        60th Venice Biennale, Venice
        Bodily Powers, Crèvecœur, Paris

Public Collections

Banco de la República, Bogotá
Essex Collection of Art from Latin America–ESCALA,
Colchester
MAMCO, Geneva
Musée d'art et d'archéologie du Périgord–MAAP,
Périgueux
Museo de Antioquia, Medellín
Museo de Arte Moderna de Bogotá–MAMBO, Bogotá
Museo de Arte Moderno La Tertulia, Cali
Museo de Arte Moderno, Barranquilla
Museo de Arte Moderno, Bucaramanga
Museo de Arte Moderno, Cartagena
Museo de Arte, Pereira
Museo Nacional de Colombia, Bogotá
Museo Rayo, Roldanillo

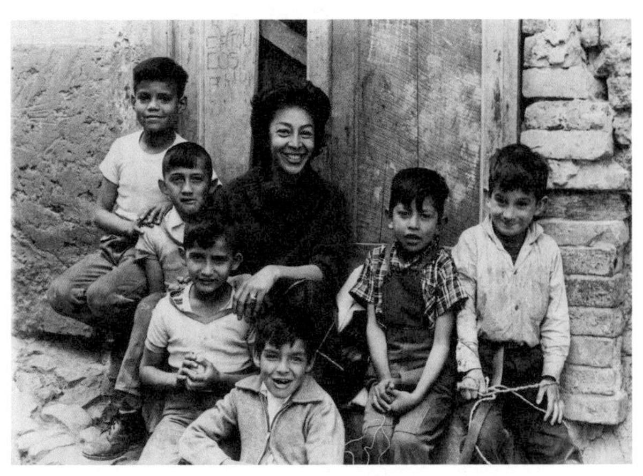

Emma Reyes surrounded by young boys on her return to
Colombia in 1961
Photograph probably taken in Bogotá's San Cristobal
neighborhood where the artist lived as a child with her
mother and sister

→

Exhibition view, Emma Reyes, MAMCO, Geneva, 2023–2024

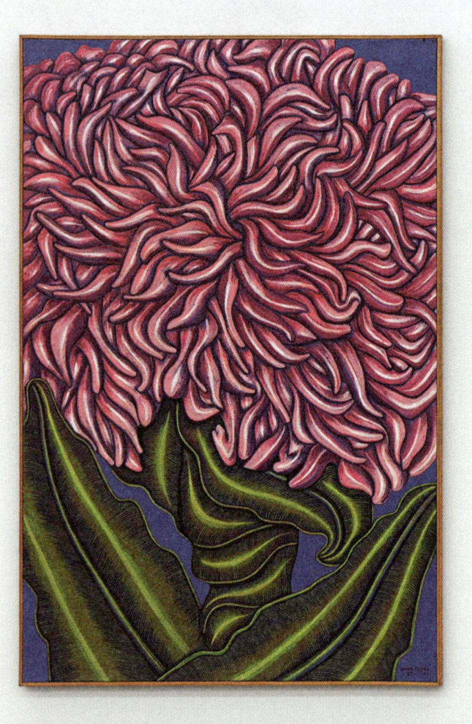

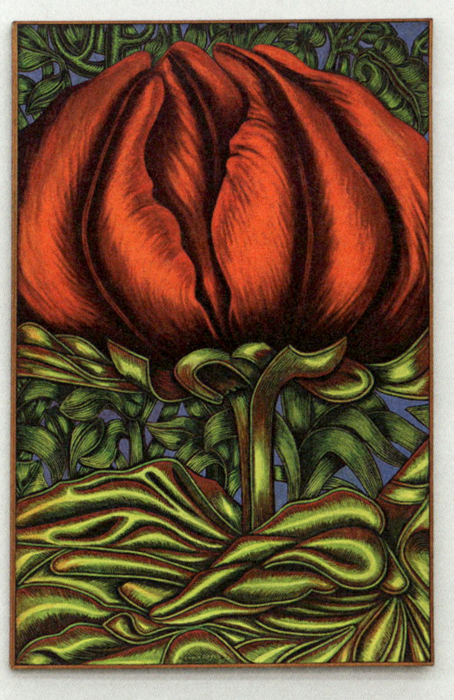

This book is published on the occasion of the exhibition *Emma Reyes* held at MAMCO Geneva from October 3, 2023, to January 28, 2024.

The exhibition was curated by Stéphanie Cottin, and received the support of the Pictet Group Foundation and the Brownstone Foundation, Paris.

MAMCO and Stéphanie Cottin would like to thank the Musée d'art et d'archéologie du Périgord, Périgueux, to which Emma Reyes entrusted the works in her studio as well as her archives in 1995, and its director Véronique Merlin-Anglade, for their collaboration.

Book published in collaboration with MAMCO Geneva.

MAMCO
GENEVE

Acknowledgments: Stéphanie Cottin would like to acknowledge Olivier Delbes, Honorary President of the Association Emma Reyes; the Association Emma Reyes; Lionel Bovier, Director, and the entire MAMCO Geneva team; the lenders: the Musée d'art et d'archéologie du Périgord, Périgueux, especially Véronique Merlin-Anglade, Isabelle Maleyre, and Myriam Grenier; Frédéric and Delphine Mohr-Durdez; Caroline and Xavier Perromat; and the enthusiastic Reyes "fan club": Ramiro Arango, Isabelle Cornaro, Jean-Matthieu Cottin, Julio Cytrangulo, Martine and Alain Deluc, Clément Dirié, Julien Eymeri, Cédric Fauq, Georges Gomez y Caceres, Sofia Gotti and Riccardo Boni, Élisabeth Lebovici, France Marquet, Peter and Marie-Léa Mohr-Durdez, Adriano Pedrosa, Massimo Prampolini, the Otero and Penagos families, Frédéric Sandoz, Louise Sartor and Élise Fourché, the Maison des Arts of Antony team; the Crèvecœur gallery; and JRP|Editions.

Collection Riccardo Boni, Rome: p. 72; Collection Julio Cytrangulo, Brazil: p. 61; Collection MAMCO, Geneva: p. 16; Collection Frédéric & Delphine Mohr-Durdez: p. 17; Collection Museo de Arte, Pereira: p. 4; Collection Caroline & Xavier Perromat: p. 29; Collection Ville de Périgueux–Musée d'art et d'archéologie du Périgord (MAAP), Périgueux: cover, p. 1, 13–15, 19–23, 25–27, 30–31, 33–35, 41, 54; Private Collection, Bordeaux: p. 52–53

Publication

Editors
STÉPHANIE COTTIN, CLÉMENT DIRIÉ

Copy Editing and Proofreading
CLARE MANCHESTER

Graphic Design
COLINE HOUOT

Color Separation and Print
MUSUMECI S.P.A., QUART (Aoste)

Typeface
HERMES (www.optimo.ch)

Cover
Untitled, 1988–1989
Acrylic paint on canvas, 130 × 96 cm

Page 72
Untitled, 1955
Oil and oil stick on canvas,
75 × 93 cm

Photo Credits
O. D'AGOSTINO: p. 59; HERNAN DIAZ:
p. 67; FELIPE FERRÉ: p. 61;
MARCELLO MAGGIORI: p. 42–43, 56,
58; GERARD MILLET: p. 64; ANNIK
WETTER: p. 1, 13–35, 41, 68–69

Printed in Europe
ISBN 978-3-03764-617-5
A French version is available under
the ISBN 978-3-03764-616-8.

Published by
JRP|Editions
Rue des Bains 39
CH–1205 Genève

JRP|Editions publications
are available internationally
at selected bookstores and
from the following distribution
partners:

SWITZERLAND
AVA Verlagsauslieferung AG
www.ava.ch

GERMANY AND AUSTRIA
JRP|Editions
books@jrp-editions.com

FRANCE
Les presses du réel
www.lespressesdureel.com

UK, EUROPEAN COUNTRIES, USA,
CANADA, ASIA AND AUSTRALIA
ARTBOOK|D.A.P.
www.artbook.com

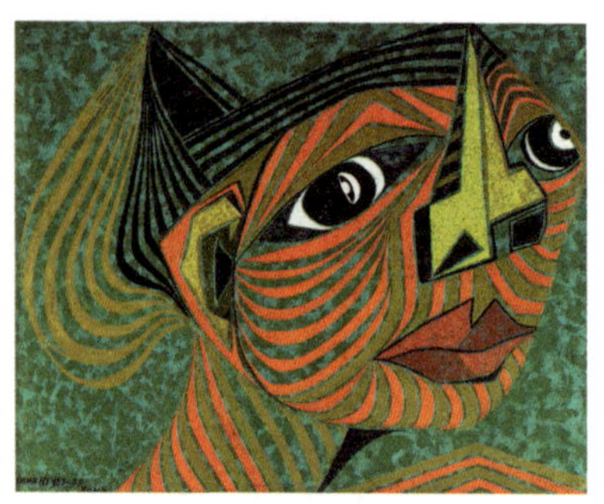

In the same series

CLÉMENT DIRIÉ (ED.)
Ana Jotta: Une chambre en ville
ISBN 978-3-03764-604-5

LIONEL BOVIER (ED.)
ECART (1969–1980)
ISBN 978-3-03764-331-0

CLÉMENT DIRIÉ (ED.)
Pierre Keller: Le Kilo-Art
ISBN 978-3-03764-544-4